Rookie
Read-About®
Science

Tadpole
to Frog

by Lisa M. Herrington

Content Consultant
Elizabeth Case DeSantis, M.A. Elementary Education
Julia A. Stark Elementary School, Stamford, Connecticut

Reading Consultant
Jeanne M. Clidas, Ph.D.
Reading Specialist

Children's Press®
An Imprint of Scholastic Inc.
New York Toronto London Auckland Sydney
Mexico City New Delhi Hong Kong
Danbury, Connecticut

Library of Congress Cataloging-in-Publication Data
Herrington, Lisa M.
   Tadpole to Frog/by Lisa M. Herrington; content consultant Elizabeth Case DeSantis,
M.A. Elementary Education, Grade 2 Teacher, Julia A. Stark Elementary, Stamford,
Connecticut; reading consultant, Jeanne Clidas, Ph.D.
      pages cm. — (Rookie read-about science)
   Includes index.
   Audience: Age 3 - 6.
   ISBN 978-0-531-21057-4 (library binding) — ISBN 978-0-531-24978-9 (pbk.)
1. Frogs—Life cycles—Juvenile literature. 2. Tadpoles—Juvenile literature. I. Title.

 QL668.E2H447 2014
 597.87—dc23   2013034815

Produced by Spooky Cheetah Press
Design by Keith Plechaty

Printed in China 62

1 2 3 4 5 6 7 8 9 10 R 23 22 21 20 19 18 17 16 15 14

Photographs © 2014: AP Images/Solent News/Rex Features: 3 top right, 29 top right;
FLPA/Treat Davidson: 23; iStockphoto/Gannet77: 24; Newscom: 20 (David Northcott/
DanitaDelimont.com), 28 inset (National News/ZUMA Press); Science Source: cover top
center, 11, 19 (Dan Suzio), cover top left, 7, 8, 26 top, 27 top, 31 center top, 31 bottom
(ER Degginger), 12, 16 (Gary Meszaros), 30 (Jim Zipp), cover top right, 15, 27 bottom
(John M. Burnley); Shutterstock, Inc.: 29 bottom, 31 top (Richard J. Green); Shutterstock, Inc.: 29 bottom
(Brian Lasenby), cover bottom, 3 top left, 3 bottom (Eric Isselee); Superstock, Inc./
Barry Mansell: 29 top left, 31 center bottom; Thinkstock: 4 (Dorling Kindersley RF), 28
background, 29 background (iStockphoto).

Table of Contents

Frog

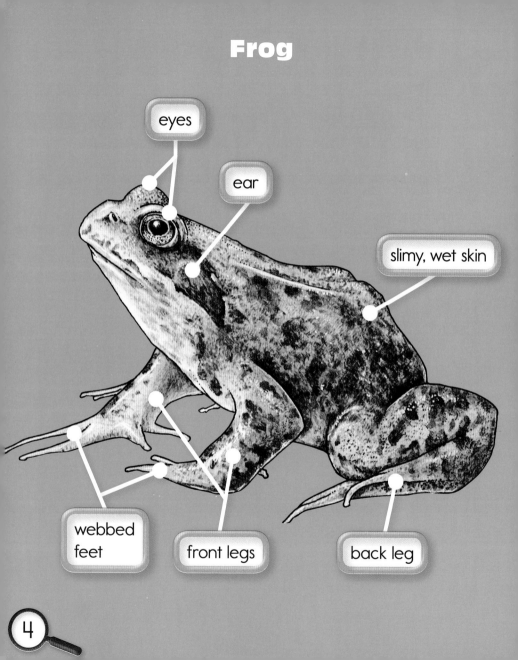

eyes

ear

slimy, wet skin

webbed feet

front legs

back leg

Amazing Amphibians

Frogs are animals that live in water and on land. They are **amphibians** (am-FIB-ee-uhns).

FUN FACT!

There are about 5,000 kinds of frogs in the world.

Laying Eggs

A frog changes as it grows. The change is called metamorphosis (met-uh-MOR-fuh-siss). It is the frog's life cycle. A frog's life cycle has three parts. It begins with a tiny black **egg**.

FUN FACT!

A soft, clear jelly surrounds each egg. It protects the egg from bumping into things.

Tadpoles on the Move

Inside the eggs, tiny **tadpoles** grow. In about a month, the tadpoles wiggle out of the eggs.

Many tadpoles hatch at the same time.

Tadpoles look like fish, but they are really baby frogs.

Tadpoles have long tails. They use them to swim. The tadpoles breathe underwater through gills.

FUN FACT!

Tadpoles are also called pollywogs.

Tadpoles eat a lot so they can grow quickly. They use their tiny teeth to chew food.

Among other things, tadpoles eat plants.

A tadpole goes through many changes. At six weeks, its back legs grow. The tadpole slowly loses its gills. Its lungs form. Now the tadpole has to swim to the top of the water to breathe air.

A tadpole's back legs help it swim fast.

front leg

back legs

tail

Next, the tadpole's front legs appear. Its tail will get shorter and shorter. The tadpole starts to look more like a frog.

This tadpole will soon lose its tail.

Frogs breathe with lungs and through their skin.

Finally, Frogs!

The tadpole is now a young frog! It might still have a small tail. When the frog is about 16 weeks old, its tail disappears. The frog is ready to live on land.

FUN FACT!

Young frogs are called froglets.

This frog leaps into the pond for a swim.

The frog stays close to water. It needs to keep its skin wet.

FUN FACT!

Frogs jump to find food or escape danger. Some frogs can leap 20 times their body length!

The adult frog uses its big eyes to find food. It catches bugs with its long, sticky tongue. Some frogs, like bullfrogs, leap at their prey and swallow it whole.

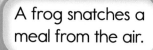

A frog snatches a meal from the air.

A mother frog lays hundreds, or even thousands, of eggs at a time.

A mother frog lays her eggs.
The life cycle begins again.

FUN FACT!

Frogs live about eight years.

A Frog's

A female frog lays eggs in water.

The tadpole loses its tail. It is now a frog.

Life Cycle

Think About It

How do frogs begin life?

What do bigger tadpoles grow?

How does a tadpole become a frog?

A tiny tadpole hatches from an egg.

A bigger tadpole grows legs.

Our world is hopping with frogs. They live near ponds and streams. Some live in trees. Others live underground. All frogs start off as eggs.

Meet the world's smallest frog. This tiny hopper is the size of a fly! It was discovered in Papua New Guinea. It is one of the few frogs that do not go through a tadpole stage.

Frogs

Poison dart frogs have bright skin. The color warns enemies not to eat them. These frogs live mainly in Central and South America.

Red-eyed tree frogs lay their eggs on the bottom of leaves that hang over ponds. The eggs hatch and the tadpoles fall into the water. They live mainly in Central America.

Let's Explore!

Croaks and peeps are just some of the noises that male frogs make. Each kind of male frog has its own sound to call to female frogs. If you have a pond nearby, listen for frog calls with an adult. If not, go online with an adult to hear some.

Food Chain

Living creatures depend on each other for their food. Plants help many creatures grow and move through their own life cycles. Some insects feed on plants. Crickets, for example, are part of a hungry frog's diet. Snakes and other animals feed on frogs. Then those small animals become food for larger animals. This is called a food chain.

Plants

Plants grow.

Cricket

A cricket eats plants.

Frog

A frog eats the cricket.

Snake

A snake feeds on the frog.

Hawk

A hawk eats the snake.

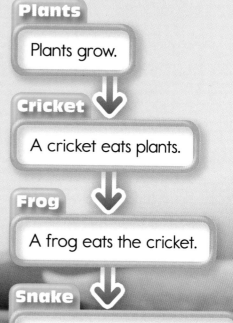

Glossary

amphibians (am-FIB-ee-uhns): animals that live in water and on land

egg (egg): the place where the tadpole grows

frogs (frawgs): small animals with webbed feet and long back legs for jumping

tadpoles (TAD-poles): young frogs that live in water and breathe through gills

Index

Facts for Now

Visit this Scholastic Web site for more information on frogs:
www.factsfornow.scholastic.com
Enter the keyword **Frogs**

About the Author

Lisa M. Herrington writes books and articles for kids. She lives in Trumbull, Connecticut, with her husband, Ryan, and daughter, Caroline. Each spring, they watch tadpoles grow into frogs at a pond near their home.